RIDERS UP!
preparing for a pony race

RIDERS UP!
preparing for a pony race

Barbara Beirne

Carolrhoda Books, Inc. / Minneapolis

Working with Jasmine and her parents, Cindy and Charles Napravnik, has been a wonderful experience. They have truly made me feel like a part of their family, and I will miss them when this book is completed. I would particularly like to thank them for being so understanding and kind to someone who's so awkward around horses. I also appreciate the time taken by Abby Shultus and Blyth Miller to explain to me the intricacies of training a pony. Judy Freer, Bob Zimmerman, and Chris Beirne were kind enough to help me on the day of the race. I'm grateful to them. Finally, I would like to thank the Far Hills Race Meeting Association, the Somerset Medical Center, and the Somerset Hills Pony Club.

The photograph on page 52 appears through the courtesy of Judy Freer, and those on pages 53 and 54 courtesy of Winners Photo.

LIBRARY OF CONGRESS CATALOGING-IN-PUBLICATION DATA

Beirne, Barbara.
    Riders up! : preparing for a pony race / by Barbara Beirne.
      p.   cm.
    Summary: Text and photographs follow eight-year-old Jasmine Napravnik through a year of physical and mental preparation for a pony race.
    ISBN 0-87614-714-7 (lib. bdg.)
    1. Ponies—Training—Juvenile literature. 2. Welsh Mountain Pony—Training—Juvenile literature. 3. Pony racing—Juvenile literature. [1. Ponies—Training. 2. Pony racing. 3. Napravnik, Jasmine Jade.] I. Title.
SF 315.B43 1992
798.4—dc20
                                                              91-38691
                                                                   CIP
                                                                    AC

Manufactured in the United States of America

1 2 3 4 5 6 7 8 9 10 01 00 99 98 97 96 95 94 93 92

My daughter, Treacy, had a wonderful pony named Hobbit when she was Jasmine's age. Their years together were filled with joy. This book is dedicated to Treacy in memory of that very special time.

I love horses. In fact, my whole family loves horses. When I was little, my mother often took me to the stable where she works, and I started to ride when I was three. I'm eight years old now. My name is Jasmine Jade Napravnik, but most people call me Jasmine or Jazz. I live with my parents, my little brother, and my little sister in High Bridge, New Jersey.

My pony's name is Sweet Sensation, but we only use that name for horse shows. Everyone calls my pony

Charlie. I named him after Charlie Brown, because he's funny. You never quite know what he's going to do next.

Charlie is a Welsh Mountain pony. These ponies are popular because they're usually very gentle.

When my mom and dad bought Charlie, he was five years old and *green broke*. That means I could ride him, but he wasn't trained enough to follow all my commands. Once Charlie is fully trained, he'll know just what I want him to do.

I'm almost exactly one year older than Charlie. He's seven years old now, and for the last two years I've schooled him. That means teaching him to understand my commands. Schooling Charlie has taken patience, but I've learned a lot from him. Charlie and I are a team. We've grown up together.

I want to do everything possible to train Charlie properly, because this is a *very* special year. This year I want to enter Charlie in a race. Each fall, children's pony races are held in Far Hills, New Jersey. The pony races are part of the Far Hills Race Meeting.

After the pony races, there are steeplechase races for grown-up jockeys and their Thoroughbred horses. Steeplechase races are really exciting. The horses have to run as fast as they can and jump over fences and hurdles. The pony races are "on the flat," which means there are no jumps.

My biggest job right now is to convince my parents that Charlie and I are ready to compete. They always worry that I'll get hurt. Mom and Dad say that they won't decide about the race until late in the summer. Dad says, "Jasmine, you know it will take hours of training to get Charlie ready. You'll have to work with him as much as you can this spring, and every day all summer. That's a big responsibility."

I know I can do it. More than anything in the world, I want to be a jockey.

Mom says she'll help me set up a training program. We keep Charlie at Windy Hill Farm, where my mom works. She teaches riding and manages the barn. My dad is a farrier, so he spends time at the barn too. A farrier is a person who shoes horses. My mom and dad know everything about horses. Mom suggests that we start by schooling Charlie in the ring three or four days a week.

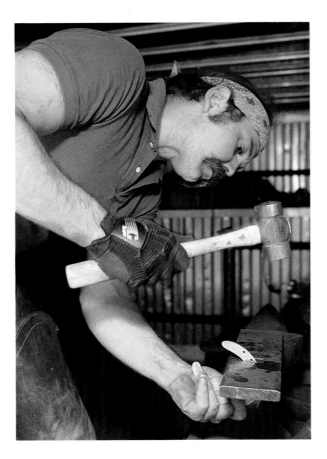

It's hard to school a pony and go to school at the same time. I have to rush home from school to groom and ride Charlie before dark. Sometimes I have to start my homework on the front steps while I wait for a ride to the barn.

As soon as I get to the barn, I saddle up Charlie and lead him out to the ring. In the ring, we work on what are called communication skills. I have to teach Charlie to respond to my signals. Most days Charlie does very well, but other times he doesn't seem to listen to me at all.

There aren't any real rules when you're schooling
a pony. Every day I decide what to do depending on
how Charlie and I feel. If Charlie is tired, I just walk
him gently around the ring so he can stretch his legs.
But when we're feeling good, we make a lot of progress.

Mom always reminds me that riding is one of the few
sports where two athletes, both the pony and the rider,
have to be in top condition. When you're going to race,
you schedule exercises so your pony is in top physical
condition at the time of the race.

I need to get in shape too. Usually when I ride, I rest my feet in stirrups, metal rings hanging down from the saddle. Today I'll ride without them. When you ride without stirrups, you have to use your legs and thighs more. This strengthens your muscles.

Training doesn't only take place in the ring. Charlie gets really bored if we do the same things all the time. He loves trail rides. They're good for him too because they help condition his body. In the spring, when Charlie hasn't had a lot of exercise, we start with short trail rides. As Charlie becomes stronger, our rides are longer. Strong lungs and heart will be important if Charlie and I race this fall.

Almost every week, I go to a meeting of the Somerset Hills Pony Club. This is part of a big organization called the United States Pony Club, Inc. I love going to these meetings, because I learn how to take care of Charlie, and I get to see my Pony Club friends. Our leaders know all about horses and they volunteer their time just to help us. Sometimes we have mounted meetings, and our whole club gets together on horseback.

15

Today's lesson is on jumping. Jumping is exciting,
but it's kind of scary.

Megan Goulart is one of my best Pony Club friends. We both started showing our ponies when we were four years old. Megan is a great rider and wins lots of blue ribbons. Even though Megan isn't interested in racing, she thinks it's wonderful that I want to be a jockey when I grow up.

Finally summer vacation starts. At last I have all the time I need to ride and get ready for the race. One of the best parts of summer is Pony Club camp, which starts in July. Our club is lucky. The United States Equestrian Team headquarters is nearby, and we rent their paddocks for our camp. Paddocks are fields surrounded by fences.

During the week of camp, there's so much to do. The most important thing for me is the class on racing techniques. If I do well in this class, maybe my parents will decide that Charlie and I can race in the fall.

The very first day
at camp, Blyth Miller, a
famous steeplechase jockey,
comes to speak. She tells
us all about racing saddles,
which are smaller and
lighter than the ones we
usually use.

Blyth started her career
as a jockey in Pony Club
races when she was nine
years old. Now she's
twenty-one and a college
student. If you want to
be a jockey, Blyth says you
have to have confidence
and determination.

The day I'm assigned to a racing class, Charlie can tell something exciting is going to happen. Our instructor, Abby Shultus, tells us first to raise our stirrups. Jockeys shorten their stirrups so they can ride as close as possible to the horse's body. This position helps the horse run faster.

Abby has us attach our crops, or sticks, to the middle finger of either hand with an elastic band. That way, we can swing the crop back and forth without worrying that it will drop to the ground. Most riders tap their horses with a crop often during races. "The crop shouldn't be used for punishment," Abby says. "Use it to keep your pony's attention."

At last it's time to run a practice race. Abby leads us across a field into a paddock. It's safer here than in an open field in case one of the ponies decides not to stop. Abby tells everyone to line up at one end of the paddock.

Racing against other ponies is hard. At first I feel like I'm flying! Then Charlie starts to run too fast. I lose my concentration and pull back roughly.

I know right away that this is wrong, and I promise myself not to let it happen again. Pulling back on the reins like this could really hurt Charlie. We communicate with each other all the time through the touch of my hands on the reins. I should only have to pull gently to signal Charlie that I want him to slow down. Riders call this keeping the feel of the pony's mouth.

Once we've raced three-eighths of a mile, Abby announces our times. It took me over a minute—longer than most of the other riders. Abby reminds me that Charlie is only twelve hands. A hand is four inches—about the same as the distance across the palm of an older person's hand. Horses and ponies are measured in "hands" from the withers, or the top of the shoulders, to the hooves. At twelve hands, Charlie is smaller than most of the other ponies.

"The bigger the pony, the longer the stride," Abby explains. Charlie can't run as fast as the larger ponies, but that's OK. Charlie and I have raced, and it was wonderful!

After camp, all I can think about is racing. The most important part of racing for a jockey is good balance. Each night after dinner, I practice balancing myself on old railroad tracks in our yard. (Trains stopped using the tracks a long time ago.) Before bedtime, I read stories about racehorses to my brother.

Even when it rains and I can't school Charlie, I go to the barn. There's always work to be done. Sometimes my little sister and brother help out, but mostly I work alone.

Charlie has to be fed. It's also important that
his stall is clean. Every day I take out the wet wood
shavings and replace them with clean shavings for his
bedding. This is called mucking out the stall. If you
leave the stall dirty and wet, your pony can get sick.

Ponies take a lot of time. I spend more time grooming Charlie and cleaning his stall than I spend riding him. You really have to love your pony to work this hard.

One Sunday afternoon in early August, after a long day at the barn, I ask my parents, "Am I doing a good enough job?"

"You're doing a great job, Jasmine," Dad says. "You've trained Charlie well. He's much more disciplined than he was just three months ago. In fact, your mom and I have decided that if Charlie continues to do well over the next three months, you can enter the race." I'm so excited I can hardly talk.

Mom has a surprise for me. Blyth Miller has invited us to visit her farm in Pennsylvania. The first thing we see at Fox Farret Farm is a beautiful stallion with his front legs in a whirlpool bath. Blyth tells us that the racehorses often swim in the pond and then have a whirlpool treatment. The cold water in the whirlpool increases blood circulation in a horse's legs.

After Blyth exercises one of the Thoroughbreds, she checks out my racing position. "You'll really have to practice this position, Jasmine. When your pony is running, his weight is forward. Your weight should be forward too, or you'll slow Charlie down," Blyth explains.

Mom talks to Blyth about our conditioning program for Charlie. Blyth agrees with what we're doing, but suggests that in October we sprint about one-quarter mile once a week.

Before we leave, I turn to Blyth and ask, "Do you ever get scared?"

"Yeah, I get scared, Jasmine," Blyth answers, "but it helps me to be careful. The day I stop being a little scared, I should probably stop racing."

The rest of the summer I spend almost all of my time at the barn. It's not all work. I have lots of fun too. My friend Katie Teiger is taking riding lessons from my mom. As soon as each lesson is over, Katie and I head to the barn. We have a secret club there. Up in the hayloft—our secret hiding place—no one can see us and we can do whatever we want.

I'm so busy working with Charlie that the days fly
by. But one day stands out—the day we order my
racing silks. Jockeys wear colorful shirts and covers
on their caps. This helps the spectators at the track
identify the horses and riders. The jackets and cap
covers used to be made of silk. Now the material is
usually nylon, but the outfits are still called racing
silks. The outfit has to be ordered, and I get to choose
the colors. It's easy for me to decide. My favorite
color is pink.

When school starts again in the fall, I ride in the late afternoon. One day Mom and I decide to try something new. Charlie has to become used to having other horses gallop close to him.

Mom brings out her horse, Danny, and we race together. Charlie behaves like a real champion. He likes having Danny around.

Four weeks before the race, the Pony Club holds a clinic to practice the start of the race. In our pony race, there isn't a starting gate. A person called the starter has the ponies form a line, and then a circle. When all the ponies are ready, the starter will shout, "TURN YOUR PONIES. GO!"

You've got to concentrate, because you never know when the starter will say the magic words. If someone has a false start, everyone has to begin again and that wastes your pony's energy. You want to have your pony in position and ready to run the second the starter says "GO!" We practice the start many, many times before we get it right. It's much harder than it sounds.

Two weeks before the race, Dad says it's time to shoe Charlie. Dad decides Charlie should have aluminum race plates on his front hooves, and light steel shoes on his rear hooves. The shoes come in different sizes, but they still have to be fitted for each horse. Dad also welds some prongs on the rear shoes. The prongs are made of borium, which is a hard metal. Prongs dig into the grass so Charlie won't slip. Soccer players wear cleats for the same reason.

Ten days before the race, Mom takes Charlie and me out to a field behind the barn for a lesson. Our plan is to start slowly by walking Charlie and end the lesson with the weekly sprint.

It's a cool day, and Charlie is spirited and hard to control. He seems determined to do things his way. As I start to gallop, Charlie bucks.

The next thing I know, I'm on the ground. Charlie knows something is wrong. He runs to the end of the field.

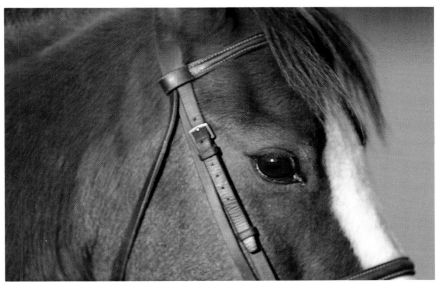

I start to cry even though I'm not really hurt. I don't have a broken bone or anything. But my feelings are hurt. I feel the way you feel when a friend disappoints you or is mean to you.

Mom checks to make certain I'm not hurt. Then she brings Charlie over to me and says, "Get back on Charlie, Jasmine, and bring him to the barn." I'm really mad at Charlie, but I do what Mom says.

When we get back to the barn, Mom and I have a talk. Mom reminds me that training a pony isn't easy, and I shouldn't be mad at Charlie. I know Charlie didn't try to scare me. He was just excited, and sometimes ponies buck when they're excited.

Mom wants me to lower the stirrups so I have more control. "You won't go as fast, but it will be safer for you, Jasmine."

I guess Mom is right. Maybe I've been pushing Charlie too hard. The next week Charlie and I just have fun and take long trail rides.

Two days before the race, my Pony Club meets at
Moorland Farms where the race will be held. Our job
is to walk the course with our parents and find any
holes hidden in the grass. These holes can be very
dangerous. If a horse or pony steps into a hole, it
might break a leg. When we find anything that looks
unsafe, we mark it with a stick. Later, the ground
crew will check the field and make certain all the
holes are filled firmly with dirt.

There are zillions of things to do the day before the race. First Charlie has to be exercised. I ride him for about 20 minutes. It's important for him to stretch his legs, but he shouldn't get too tired. Charlie knows something big is going to happen.

I spend hours grooming him. Charlie is starting to grow his winter coat, so Mom helps me by using an electric clipper. Since Charlie is going to spend the winter in a stable, we don't want his coat to grow too long. After I'm certain Charlie looks perfect, I put him in his stall.

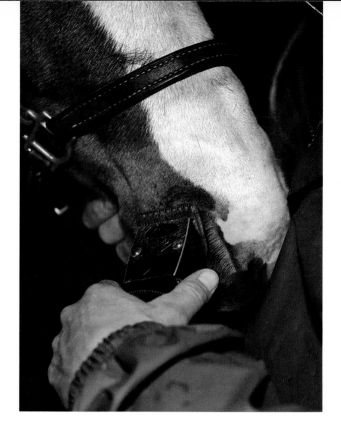

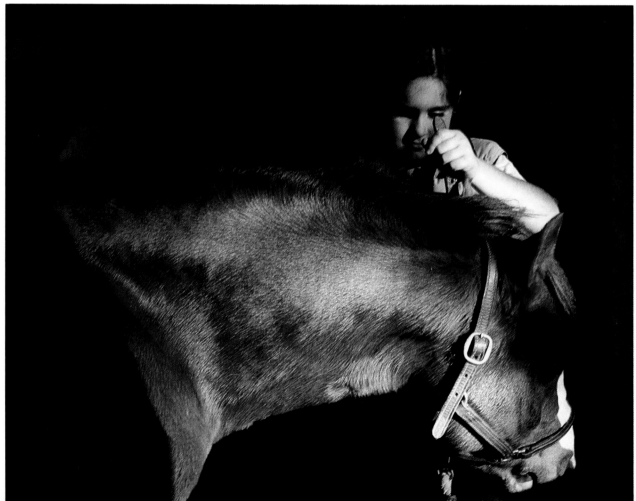

Next I have to clean every piece of equipment I'll be using in the race. The leather pieces, called tack, need to be cleaned, washed, and then rubbed with a special paste. At a Pony Club meeting, we learned that the stitching on the leather has to be checked. If the stitching is weak or torn, it could break. During a race, your pony's tack is under more pressure than when you're riding for fun. Broken tack can cause serious accidents!

One thing worries me. Dark storm clouds are coming
in. The weather reports all say we're going to have rain.
If it rains, the race will still be held, but the course
could be muddy and slippery. Will Mom and Dad let
me ride if the conditions aren't good? Should I ride
on a slippery course, or would it be too dangerous for
Charlie?

On the day of the race, my alarm clock goes off at
6:00 A.M. I keep my eyes closed and listen for rain.
Everything's quiet. When I look out the window, the
sun is beginning to rise. I give Charlie breakfast at
the barn, and we're ready to go. After all our work,
Charlie and I are going to race.

When we arrive at Moorland Farms, there are thousands of people, horses, vans, trucks, tents, and balloons. Steeplechase and pony races are like big parties. Spectators sit on the grass next to the course. Many people bring picnics and decorate their cars.

ENTRANCE
FAR HILLS
RACE MEETING
—
MOORLAND FARMS
FAR HILLS, N.J.

NO
RKING

Mom warns me not to be distracted by all the con-
fusion. We walk the three-eighths-of-a-mile course
one last time. Since the track is grass, it looks like
an open field. The course splits when we go up the
hill, and it would be easy to take a wrong turn.
Wouldn't that be embarrassing!

We still have one more hour until the race. Mom
doesn't want me to get dressed too early. I know she
thinks I'll get my new silks dirty, but I can't wait
another minute. I'm starting to get a little nervous.

Since we still have a little time to wait, I leave Charlie and go to the tent where the Thoroughbred racehorses are kept. Bill Jones, a groom, gives me some advice. "Make sure to take care of your pony after the race, Jasmine," he says.

After any type of exercise, a pony needs to be cooled out. When I cool out Charlie, I walk him on a lead rope until his temperature is back to normal and he stops sweating. Bill tells me that some racehorses need a full hour for cooling out after a hard race. Charlie won't take that much time, since the pony race is short. Bill also reminds me to allow Charlie only a few sips of water until he's cool. Too much water or feed could make him sick.

The official racing program arrives. I thought only
the steeplechase races would be listed, but my pony
race, officially called the Junior Fox Hunter's Race for
Small Ponies, is included. It's great to see my name
listed with the other jockeys. I'm assigned number
three — my lucky number. Charlie's show name, Sweet
Sensation, is also on the program.

Finally it's time for the race. Mom, my groom for the day, leads Charlie to the paddock. I don't think I've ever been as excited as I am at this very minute. I can feel my heart pounding as we crowd into the paddock.

When all the riders and ponies are ready, the paddock judge shouts, "RIDERS UP!" Mom gives me a "leg up" and says, "Have a great time, Jazz. You and Charlie earned it."

We hear the sound of the horn warning that the race is about to begin. All 11 riders line up for the parade to the starting area. Outriders—grown-ups who are not in this race—lead the parade. They also help control the crowd and catch any stray ponies.

I can hardly wait for the race to start. I have butter-
flies in my stomach, but Charlie seems as calm as a
seasoned racing pony. I want Charlie to start at a
gallop, so he has to be able to stretch his head out
on the first few strides. At the last second, I'll reach
out and hold onto his mane for control instead of short-
ening the reins. I'm not going to be left behind.

When the starter says "GO!," we're ready. We get
off to a great start. I keep talking to Charlie as we
fly along. "You're doing a great job. Just do the best
you can."

Some of the larger ponies pass us, but Charlie is running faster than he ever has before. He's also responding to all of my commands. I couldn't ask for more.

As we start up the final hill and into the home stretch, I touch Charlie with the crop. "Give it all you can, boy!"

And he does just that.

Charlie runs a great race. As we cross the finish line,
we can hear the crowd cheering. We come in seventh,
but we manage to run the race in under a minute,
which is the best we've ever done.

I congratulate my friend Veda, who is the winner.
Then I ask permission to dismount by touching my cap
with my crop. The judge has to nod approval.

After the race, there's so much
excitement. Photographers crowd
around to take our picture. My family
is there to congratulate me and Charlie.
Mom and Dad are as happy as I am.

"We're so proud of you," Dad says. "You really worked hard for this, Jazz."

"No Dad, *we* worked hard for this," I answer. I give Charlie one more hug before going to cool him out. As we head to the trailer, I turn back and call to the judge, "We'll see you next year!"